I'M GOING TO SING

I'M GOING TO SING

BLACK AMERICAN SPIRITUALS   volume two

selected and illustrated by

Ashley Bryan

Atheneum   1984   New York

ISBN 0-689-30915-5

Copyright © 1982 by Ashley Bryan
All rights reserved
Published simultaneously in Canada by
McClelland & Stewart, Ltd.
Composition by Dix Type, Inc., Syracuse, New York
Printed and bound by Kingsport Press
Kingsport, Tennessee
First Printing September 1982
Second Printing December 1984

Contents

Introduction   vii

When the Saints   3

Steal Away   5

Joshua Fit the Battle   6

In-a That Morning   9

I'm Going to Sing   11

Old Time Religion   12

I Know the Lord   15

Weary Traveler   17

Every Time I Feel the Spirit   18

Motherless Child   21

Hail! Hail! Hail!   23

The Gospel Train   24

By and By   29

It's Me O Lord   31

Study War No More   32

You Shall Reap   35

Somebody's Knocking   37

I'm A-Rolling   38

Do Lord Remember Me   41

Rise Up Shepherd & Follow   43

Father Abraham   45

You Got a Right   47

My Lord What a Morning   49

O Mary Don't You Weep   50

Many Thousand Gone   53

To the Memory of my Brother
Sidney
In-a That Morning

I'M GOING TO SING

"I'm going to sing when the spirit says sing
And obey the spirit of the Lord."

My earliest childhood recollections are of my mother singing. She sang from one end of the day to the other. My father used to say, "Son, your mother must think she's a bird."

For his part, my father loved birds. Although his earnings as a printer were modest and there were six children to support, he couldn't resist buying birds. The living rooms of our various Bronx apartments were always lined with shelves, not for books, but for birds. At one time I counted over a hundred birds in his collection. My mother used to say, "If I want any attention around here I'd have to get into a cage."

My father played a number of instruments; saxaphone, guitar, banjo, and there was always a piano in the house. On Sundays he was often visited by his boyhood friends. They had all come to New York from Antigua in the West Indies soon after World War I. They had a great time playing music as they had done on the island, exchanging instruments and reminiscences as they went along.

With the birds trilling, my mother singing and the general music-making that went on at home, I cannot recall when I first distinguished the spirituals from the other music. But these songs took root in me early because of their rhythmic appeal and beauty.

I cannot remember a time when I was not drawing and painting, and the spirituals played a role in that growth. I began to recognize images for these songs in almost everything I saw. Or they stimulated my efforts to draw pictures of what can only be seen through the imagination. I have often done drawings that came right out of these songs. It was natural, then, that I would one day begin work illustrating the spirituals.

When I looked for books devoted solely to selections of these songs to offer as gifts to family and friends, I was astonished to find there were none! One does find a few of the more familiar spirituals in popular folk song books, but this hardly touches upon the hundreds of spirituals that exist.

The Black American spirituals are unique among the folk songs of the world. In a 1926 collection, *Seventy Negro Spirituals*, William Fisher wrote: "In common with other folk the Negro has his game songs, work songs, social songs, lullabies and ballads together with his own 'corn songs,' 'reel tunes' and 'devil songs,' but search the world over and nowhere can be found such a rich and spontaneous outpouring of religious song and fervor as in the spirituals of the Afro-American."

The spirituals came out of the ordeal of slavery, but each song probably began as the work of a talented individual among the Black people. Once a new song was begun, it was taken up and changed and added to as it passed on its way from area to area. The initial authors are unknown. The slaves used Biblical themes to express their experiences in songs ranging from sorrowful to joyous emotions. These songs were passed down through generations of singing Blacks who kept them alive until their worth was noted and efforts made to preserve them.

Initially specific spirituals took root locally, then spread across whole states and the entire country. Today these songs are loved and sung throughout the world and are considered America's finest contribution to world music.

In my travels abroad, I have always sought out the folk songs of the countries I visited. I have never had trouble finding varied presentations from which to choose. Native artists and musicians in their maturity, having grown up with their songs, have wanted to offer selections and illustrations of their folk songs done in their own way.

It is for this reason that each year we entertain new versions of Mother Goose, fairy tales, folk tales, alphabet and counting books. We seem never to tire of new presentations of old favorites. On the contrary, we look forward to them.

I feel that the Black American spirituals deserve this attention and varied treatment as well. When the composer, Anton Dvořák came to America in 1892, he was so impressed by the distinctive character of the spirituals that he used their melodic inspiration in a number of his compositions. He asked: "What songs, then, belong to the American? What melody would stop him on the street if he were in a strange land and make the home-feeling well up within him? The most potent, as well as the most beautiful among them, according to my estimation, are certain of the so-called plantation melodies and slave songs."

Several years ago I did my first selection of these songs in the book, *Walk*

Together Children. I chose to illustrate these songs in the spirit of the early religious block-printed books. The religious fervor of the people that inspired Western art of that period is echoed centuries later in the profound religiosity of the enslaved Black, which found creative expression in these songs. I hoped my book would have the resonance of this association. So when the illustrations were completed, I cut the titles for the songs. I then worked out a system for cutting and printing the music as well. This gave the work the visual unity I sought.

Since the spirituals were sung for generations before they were noted down, many variations may occur in melody, rhythm and words of certain songs. In choosing a final form to print for each song, I make no presumption that this is the only way the song is sung. I was, at times, hard put to choose among differing versions of a song and my way of singing it. I would try the variations over and over again on my wooden flute before deciding.

I used the C recorder to help note the melodies. It is a handy, inexpensive flute and many young people have learned to read music by means of this instrument. Most of the songs selected are within the range of the C recorder. Certainly they can be played on any other melodic instrument as well and then sung in the key most comfortable to the individual voice.

My aim then is to open these songs to further use and discovery and to encourage people to make the changes and additions they enjoy most as they become more familiar with the songs. It is in this spirit that they were created and have endured.

The spirituals are testimony to the genius of the enslaved Blacks that allowed them to remain human and creative through adversity. We stand today in the light of this achievement. The spirituals offer this precious stance and heritage as an inspiration to all people.

When we were both quite little, my older brother Sidney, to whose memory I have dedicated this book, was often put in charge of me. Although he was hardly two years older than I, we were quite different. He was quick and athletic. I was already lost in the wonders of drawing. "You take your brother with you," my mother would say as he was about to race off. "Oh, Mama!" he would reply, "he's so slow."

It is now eight years since *Walk Together Children* first appeared. It is still out there alone. At last I send out this companion to join it, *I'm Going To Sing*.

Sidney, whose habit of discreet watchfulness over me stayed with him through life, used to stop by my Bronx studio often. He enjoyed seeing the progress of my work and he understood what went into the making of it. Of that he would not have said, "Oh, Mama, he's so slow!"

I plan to continue my work, selecting from this generous gift of spirituals that Black Americans have offered to all of us. Perhaps it will not take another eight years before my next book of spirituals appears.

Come, join me now, for . . .
I'm going to sing!

Ashley Bryan, March 1982

WHEN THE SAINTS

O when the saints go march-ing in, O when the
saints go march-ing in, O Lord I want to be in that
num-ber, When the saints go march-ing in.

2. O when the sun re-fuse to shine, etc.
3. O when the moon goes down in blood, etc.
4. O when the stars have disappeared, etc.
5. O when they crown Him Lord of all, etc.

STEAL AWAY

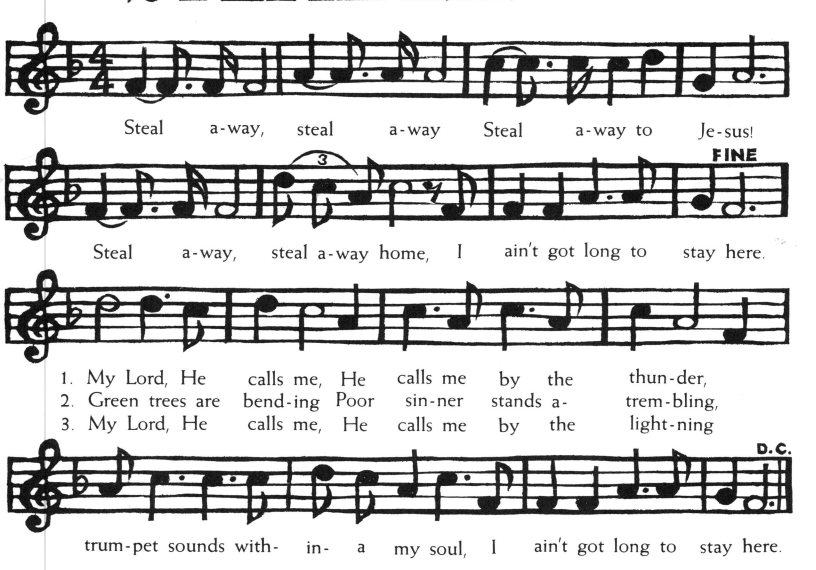

Steal a-way, steal a-way Steal a-way to Je-sus!

Steal a-way, steal a-way home, I ain't got long to stay here.

FINE

1. My Lord, He calls me, He calls me by the thun-der,
2. Green trees are bend-ing Poor sin-ner stands a- trem-bling,
3. My Lord, He calls me, He calls me by the light-ning

D.C.

trum-pet sounds with- in- a my soul, I ain't got long to stay here.

5

JOSHUA FIT THE BATTL[E]

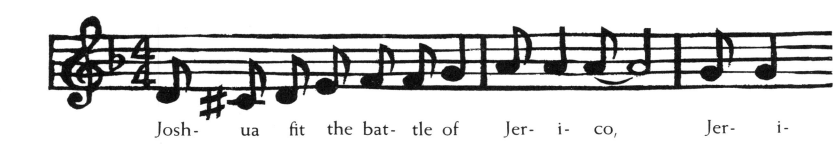

Josh- ua fit the bat- tle of Jer- i- co, Jer- i-

co, Jer- i- co, Josh- ua fit the bat- tle of

FINE

Jer- i- co, And the walls come tum- bling down.

1. You may   talk a- bout your king of Gid- e- on,   You may
       to   the   walls of Jer- i- co,   They
     lamb   ram sheep horns be-gin to blow,   The

talk a-bout your man of   Saul, But there's none like good old
marched with   spear in hand, "Go   blow   them ram horns,"
trum- pets   be- gin to   sound, Old   Josh-ua com-man-ded the

Josh- ua, At the   bat-tle of Jer- i- co. 2. Up
Josh-u a cried " 'Cause the bat-tle is in my hand." 3. Then the
chil-dren to shout, And the walls come tum-bling   down. That morn-ing.

7

IN-A THAT MORNING

1. You may bur-y me in the East, You may bur-y me
2. Good old Chris-tians in that day, They'll take wings and

in the West, But I'll hear the trum-pet sound In- a that
fly a- way For to hear the trum-pet sound In- a that

morn-ing. In- a that morn-ing my Lord, How I long to go,

For to hear the trum-pet sound In- a that morn-ing.

I'M GOING TO SING

I'm going to sing when the spir-it says sing I'm going to
pray pray
shout shout

sing when the spir-it says sing I'm going to sing when the spir-it says
pray pray pray
shout shout shout

sing And o-bey the spir-it of the Lord.
pray
shout

OLD TIME RELIGION

Give me that old time re- li-gion, Give me that old time re-

li-gion, Give me that old time re- li-gion, It's good e-nough for

me. Just give me that old time re- li-gion Give me that

old time re- li-gion, Give me that old time re- li-gion, It's

good e-nough for me. It was good for the He-brew child-ren, It was
do when the world's on fi – re, It will

good for the He-brew child-ren, It was good for the He-brew child-ren
do when the world's on fi – re, It will do when the world's on fi – re,

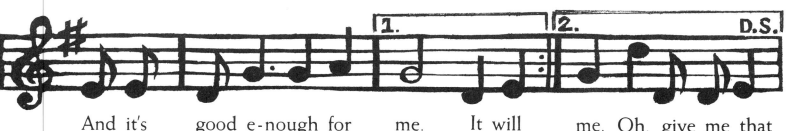

And it's good e-nough for me. It will me. Oh, give me that
And it's good e-nough for

I KNOW THE LORD

O   I know the   Lord,   I know the   Lord,   I know the

Lord's laid his   hands on me;   1. Did   ev-er   you see the   like be-fore?
Je-   sus preach-ing to the poor?
2. O   was-   n't that   a   hap-py day,
Je-   sus washed my sins a-   way?
3. Some seek   the Lord and don't seek him right,
fool   all day and   pray at night,

I know the   Lord's laid his   hands on me, King   hands on   me. O
When
They

WEARY TRAVELLER

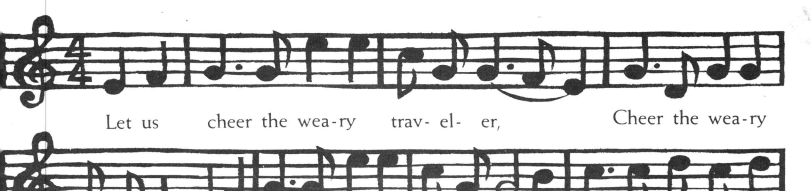

Let us   cheer the wea-ry   trav- el- er,   Cheer the wea-ry

trav-el- er. Let us cheer the wea-ry trav- el- er A- long the heav-en- ly

FINE

way.   1. I'll   take my gos-pel   trum-pet, And   I'll   be-gin   to   blow,
     2. And   if you meet with   cross-es And   tri- als on   the   way,
     3. If you can-not sing like   An-gels,   If you can-not pray   like Paul,

D.C.

And   if   my Sav-iour helps me,   I'll   blow wher-ev   er   I   go.
Just   keep your trust in   Je-sus,   And don't for- get   to   pray.
You can tell the love of   Je-sus   And   say He died   for   all.

EVERY TIME I FEEL THE SPIRIT

Ev-ery time I feel the Spir-it Mov-ing in my heart

I will pray. Ev-ery time I feel the Spir-it Mov-ing

in my heart I will pray. Up-on the moun-tain
round me
riv- er

my Lord spoke, Out His mouth came fire and smoke.
looks so shine, Ask my Lord if all was mine.
chil-ly and cold, Chills the bod-y but not the soul.

Ev – ery time I feel the Spir – it Mov -ing. in my heart

I will pray. Ev – ery time I feel the Spir-it Mov-ing

1.   **D.S.** **2.** **FINE**

in my heart I will pray. 2. All- a-   pray
               3. Jor- dan

19

MOTHERLESS CHILD

Some-times I feel like a moth-er-less child. Some-times I feel like a
Some-times I feel like I'm al-most gone, Some-times I feel like I'm

moth-er-less child, Some-times I feel like a moth-er-less child, A
al-most gone, Some-times I feel like I'm al- most gone, Way

long ways from home, — A long ways from home. True
up in the hea-ven-ly land, — Way up in the hea-ven- ly land. True

be- liev- er A long ways from home, — A long ways from home.
be- liev- er, Way up in the hea-ven-ly land, — Way up in the hea-ven-ly land.

HAIL! HAIL! HAIL!

Chil-dren hail! hail! hail! I'm go-ing to join the saints a-bove,

Hail! hail! hail! I'm on my jour-ney home. 1. O, look up

yon-der what I see I'm on my jour-ney home, Bright an-gels

com-ing af-ter me, I'm on my jour-ney home.

2. If you get there be-fore I do
Look out for me I'm com-ing too,

3. O hal-le-lu-jah to the Lamb!
King Je-sus died for ev-ery man,

THE GOSPEL TRAIN

Get on board, lit- tle chil-dren, Get on board, lit-tle chil-dren,

Get on board, lit-tle chil-dren, There's room for man-y a more. The

Gos- pel train's a com-ing, I see it close at hand, I
hear the train a com-ing, She's com-ing round the curve, She's
fare is cheap and all can go, The rich and poor are there, No

hear the car wheels rum-bling,   And   roll-ing through the   land. Get on
loos-ened all her   steam and brakes, And   strain-ing   ev-ery   nerve.
sec - ond class a   board this train, No   dif-ference   in the   fare.

board, lit- tle   chil-dren, Get on   board, lit- tle   chil-dren, Get on

1.   **2. FINE**

board, lit-tle   chil-dren, There's room for man-y a   more. 2. I   more
    3. The

25

BY AND BY

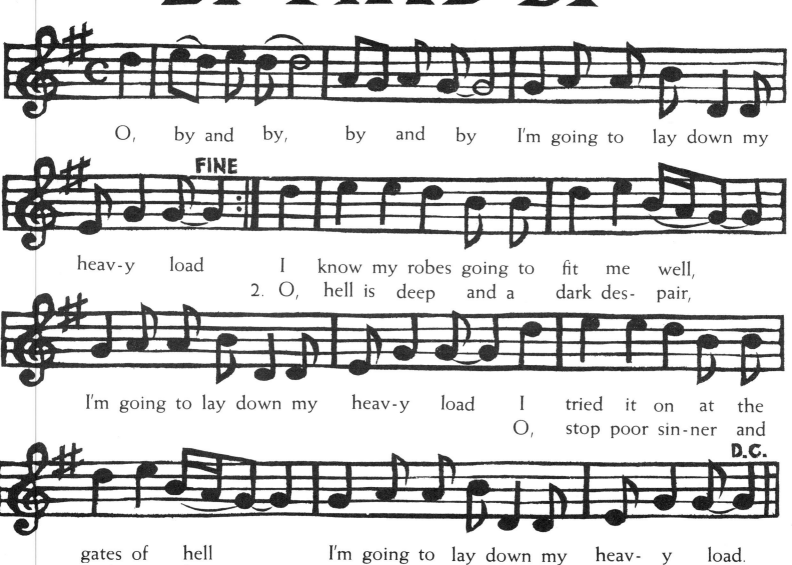

O, by and by, by and by I'm going to lay down my

FINE

heav-y load I know my robes going to fit me well,
2. O, hell is deep and a dark des-pair,

I'm going to lay down my heav-y load I tried it on at the
O, stop poor sin-ner and

D.C.

gates of hell I'm going to lay down my heav- y load.
don't go there,

IT'S ME O LORD

It's   me,   it's   me,   it's   me,   O   Lord,   Standing   in   the   need   of   prayer,

It's   me,   it's   me,   it's   me,   O   Lord   Standing   in   the   need   of   prayer.

Not   my   1.   fa-ther   not   my   mo-ther,   but   it's   me,   O   Lord,
         2.   sis-ter   not   my   bro-ther,

Standing   in   the   need   of   prayer,   Not   my   Standing   in   the   need   of   prayer.

STUDY WAR NO MORE

Going to   lay down my bur-den Lord,   Down by the   ri-ver-side
lay down my sword and shield,
put on   my long white robe,
put on   my star-ry crown,
talk with the Prince of Peace,

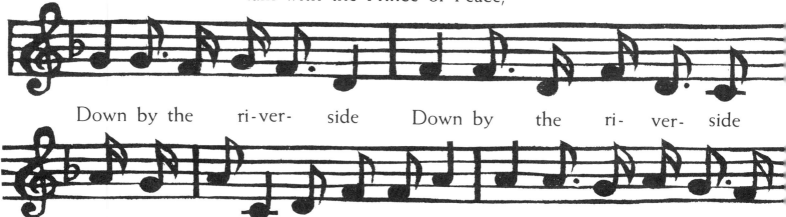

Down by the   ri-ver-   side   Down by   the   ri-   ver-   side

Going to   lay down my bur-den Lord,   Down by the   ri-   ver-side
lay down my sword and shield,
put on   my long white robe,
put on   my star- ry crown,
talk with the Prince of Peace,

Ain't going to stud- y war no more! Ain't going to

stud-y war no more Ain't going to stud-y war no more Ain't going to

stud- y war no more, no more Ain't going to stud-y war no more

Ain't going to stud-y war no more Ain't going to stud- y war no more!

33

YOU SHALL REAP

You shall reap just what you sow, You shall

reap what you sow, On the moun tain, in the

val- ley, You shall reap just what you sow.

SOMEBODY'S KNOCKING

Some-bod-y's knock-ing at your door, Some-bod-y's knock-ing at your

door, O sin-ner, why don't you an-swer? Some-bod-y's knock-ing

at your door. Knocks like Je-sus Some-bod-y's knock-ing at your
        2. Can't you hear Him?
        3. An-swer Je-sus,

door, Knocks like Je-sus, Some-bod-y's knock-ing at your door,
Can't you hear Him?
An- swer Je-sus,

I'M A-ROLLING

I'm a- roll-ing, I'm a- roll-ing, I'm a- roll-ing

through an un- friend-ly world, I'm a- roll-ing, I'm a-

roll- ing, through an un- friend-ly world.

1. O broth-ers, won't you help me, O broth-ers, won't you help me,
2. O sis- ters, O sis- ters,

to pray? O broth-ers, won't you   help me, Won't you   help me   in
O   sis- ters,

the   ser-vice   of   the   Lord?   I'm   a-   roll-ing,   I'm   a-

roll-ing,   I'm   a-   roll-ing   through an   un-   friend-ly world,   I'm a-

FINE

roll-ing, I'm   a-   roll-ing, through an   un-   friend-ly   world.

D.S. al FINE

39

DO LORD REMEMBER ME

1. Do Lord,   O   do Lord,   Do re-mem-ber me, O   Lord,
2. When I'm in   trou-ble,
3. When I'm   dy-ing,
4. When this world's on fire,

Do Lord, O do Lord,   Do re-mem-ber me,   Do Lord, O   do Lord
When I'm in trou ble,   When I'm in   trou ble,
When I'm   dy-ing,   When I'm   dy-ing,
When this world's on fire,   When this world's on fire,

Do re-mem-ber me, O,   Do Lord re-mem-ber   me.

RISE UP SHEPHERD & FOLLOW

1. There's a star in the East on Christ-mas morn,
 take good heed to the an- gel's words,

Rise up shep-herd and fol-low, It will lead to the place
 You'll for- get your flocks,

where the Sav-iour's born, —
You'll for- get your herds, — Rise up shep-herd and fol-low.

Leave your flocks and leave your lambs, Rise up shep-herd and

fol-low, fol-low, Leave your sheep and leave your rams, Rise up

shep-herd and fol-low, yes, fol-low. Fol- low, fol- low,

rise up shep-herd and fol-low Fol- low the star of

Beth-le-hem, — Rise up shep-herd and fol- low. If you fol- low.

44

FATHER ABRAHAM

Fa-ther A- bra-ham Sit- ting down side of the Hol-y Lamb.

1. 'Way up on- a the moun-tain top, My Lord he spoke and the
2. Good-bye moth-er and fare you well, Meet me a-round that

char-iot stop. Sit-ting down side of the Hol-y Lamb. Fa-ther
throne of God.

A- bra- ham Sit- ting down side of the Hol-y Lamb.

YOU GOT A RIGHT

You got a right, I got a right We all got a

right, to the tree of life. Yes, tree of life. The ve-ry

hin-der me

time I thought I was lost The dun-geon shook and the

here But you can- not there, 'Cause God in the heav-en going to

chain fell off. You may ans-wer prayer O bre-ther-en

MY LORD WHAT A MORNING

My Lord, what a morn-ing! My Lord, what a morn-ing! O

My Lord, what a morn-ing, When the stars be-gin to fall! You'll

hear the trum- pet sound, To wake the na-tions un-der ground,
2. hear the sin- ner moan,
3. hear the Chris- tian shout,

Look-ing to my God's right hand, When the stars be-gin to fall.

O MARY DON'T YOU WEEP

O Ma- ry don't you weep, don't you mourn, O Ma- ry,

don't you weep, don't you mourn; Pha-raoh's ar- my got drown-ded,

O Ma- ry, don't you weep.

1. Ain't been to Heav-en
2. Je- sus done
3. When I get to Heav-en
4. When I get to Heav-en

but I've been told: Streets is pearl and the
just as He said, He heal the sick and He
going to sing and shout, No- bod- y there for to
going to put on my shoes, Run a-bout glo-ry and

hous-es is gold, Pha-raoh's ar- my got drown-ded,
raise the dead.
turn me out.
tell all the news.

O Ma- ry, don't you weep.

MANY THOUSAND GONE

1. No more auc-tion block for me, No more, No more,

No more auc-tion block for me, Ma-ny thou-sand gone.

2. No more peck of corn for me, etc.

3. No more driver's lash for me, etc.

4. No more pint of salt for me, etc.

5. No more hundred lash for me, etc.

6. No more mistress call for me, etc.